WE ALL HAVE AN INNER ADVENTURER.

EXPLORE THE POSSIBILITIES WITH
IMAGINE PROMOTIONAL GROUP.

imagine
PROMOTIONAL GROUP

365 WAYS TO

GO WILD

EMBRACE YOUR INNER ADVENTURER
EVERY DAY OF THE YEAR

SAM LACEY

summersdale

365 WAYS TO GO WILD

An Hachette UK Company
www.hachette.co.uk

Summersdale Publishers Ltd
Part of Octopus Publishing Group Limited
Carmelite House
50 Victoria Embankment
LONDON
EC4Y 0DZ
UK

www.summersdale.com

Printed and bound in China

ISBN: 978-1-78783-678-5

Disclaimer: Neither the author nor the publisher can be held responsible for any loss or claim arising out of the use, or misuse, of the suggestions made herein.

INTRODUCTION

Nature surrounds us every day, even in cities, but often we walk by it unnoticed. While being essential for us to live, it is also inspiring and invigorating, and it's time we took more notice of it. Be intrigued by the bee that works hard, buzzing from flower to flower; feel relaxed by the rush of water at the beach or inland; and find peace as you watch clouds scud past overhead.

This book is a celebration of nature and all things wild, and takes you on a tour through different landscapes, from forest to field and sea to stream, offering ideas and activities to guide you on an unforgettable outdoor adventure. You'll be able to savour the small, precious moments of nature throughout the year with ideas for all the family, or if you prefer something even more wild, there is ample inspiration to get your adrenaline pumping.

It's time to step away from the comforts of the home and be energized by what this beautiful planet has to offer.

01

Start off your wild adventure by **FOREST BATHING**. Spend time among trees, breathe in the fresh air and notice the shafts of sunshine breaking through the rustling leaves overhead. Use this time to connect with your surroundings and feel grounded.

02

Go **ROCK-POOLING**. Find out when the tide is out and make your way to the nearest beach. Take protective footwear and gloves in case you come across wildlife that nips or stings and carry a notepad or sketchbook with you to write about or draw your finds. Don't forget to leave the rock pools behind exactly as you found them.

03

If you're out walking and happen upon a stream or river with a bridge over it, take a few moments to stand on it and WATCH THE RUSHING WATER UNDERFOOT. Let your mind be at peace.

04

On a clear night, go STARGAZING. Research constellations you are likely to see in your hemisphere and locate a spot where there's little light pollution. Feel humbled and inspired by how vast the universe is.

05

If you've had a stressful day, DON'T STAY INDOORS. Let the fresh air outside cleanse your mind and body, even if you just take a short trip to the local park.

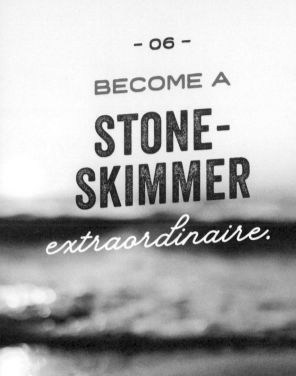

- 06 -

BECOME A

STONE-
SKIMMER

extraordinaire.

⊳━► **07** ◄━⊲

While away a couple of hours on a summer's afternoon by finding your own patch of grass, lying down and **WATCHING THE CLOUDS DRIFT OVERHEAD**. Have some fun trying to find shapes of animals, objects or people. Maybe you could challenge a friend to see who can spot the most?

08

Do some research to find out *what certain types of clouds mean* for the weather. For example, cirrus clouds (the thin, wispy kind that you see high in the sky) often mean that pleasant weather is on the way.

⊱⟶ 09 ⟵⊰

You don't need a fancy camera to take beautiful nature shots; most smartphones now have great image resolution. Look for interesting angles to make your pictures stand out – for example, you could get down on the ground and take pictures of flowers, plants or trees from underneath. Don't be put off if it's raining; water droplets catching the light can MAKE FOR A STUNNING PHOTOGRAPH.

⊱⟶ 10 ⟵⊰

VOLUNTEER TO PLANT TREES OR BUILD ANIMAL SHELTERS in your local neighbourhood or public park. There are usually lots of community groups looking for people willing to pitch in.

Do a
CARTWHEEL
IN A MEADOW.

12

If you're searching for an adrenaline hit,
try a **BUNGEE JUMP**. The view will be incredible;
but this is not for the faint-hearted!

13

It's really important to *consult a professional*, take
life-saving equipment, or have some lessons before
attempting any kind of potentially dangerous
activity. Bungee jumping, for example, should always
be arranged through a reputable company that will
put safety first, leaving you to experience the rush.

14

If you like spending time on the water,
RENT A KAYAK OR A CANOE. Take it out on the
sea or a lake, or navigate the twists and turns
of the rapids as you paddle down a river.

➣→ **15** ←⤛

BUILDING AN OBSTACLE COURSE is a fun and inexpensive activity for people with creative minds! You can use your own outside space, or find a local area and use all natural materials. If you use a public space, make sure you take everything with you when you're done.

➣→ **16** ←⤛

Whether on the beach, in a park, or simply your own backyard, take off your shoes and **FEEL THE SOFT SAND OR GRASS UNDER YOUR FEET.** Enjoy the connection to the earth beneath you.

☛ 17 ☚

PADDLE IN THE OCEAN when you get the chance. There's something so freeing about standing on the shore as the waves lap gently at your feet, looking out into the distant horizon and the deeper water beyond.

☛ 18 ☚

CLIMB A TREE to recapture your inner child and see the world from a different perspective. Make sure you can get down as easily as you got up, and consider having someone nearby to help you if you get stuck.

☛ 19 ☚

Venture out to the park with a friend and **TAKE A FRISBEE.** Practise your technique and see how far you can throw it.

☞ **20** ☜

Many productions are now staged outside in the evenings of the warmer months. If you're a fan of the arts, take your own chair and a picnic and **RELAX UNDER THE STARS** while you enjoy the show.

☞ **21** ☜

If you're lucky enough to have a tree in your garden, repurpose an old tyre and **BUILD YOURSELF A ROPE SWING**. Make sure you choose a branch that's sturdy enough to take the weight of an adult, though. Enjoy the breeze through your hair and on your face as you glide back and forth.

⇒ 22 ⇐

Instead of letting out a sigh when you see
FRESH SNOWFALL, embrace it. Put on warm clothes,
build a snowman, make a snow angel or start
a friendly neighbourhood snowball battle.

⇒ 23 ⇐

GET ARTY in nature. Paint some rocks with
colourful images and patterns, then hide them
around your local area for others to discover.

⇒ 24 ⇐

On a blustery day, head out to an open
space and **FLY A KITE**. Enjoy the excitement
of controlling it as it flutters on the breeze.
However, remember that it's important not to
fly a kite when there is a storm approaching or
in a place that's anywhere near power lines.

– 25 –

Put on some old shoes

AND
SPLASH

IN A PUDDLE!

⤞ 26 ⤝

Next time you're at the coast, take inspiration from **SAND SCULPTURE** artists and try your hand at fashioning your own. Remember to apply sun lotion regularly if it's a sunny day as this activity could take some time to perfect.

⤞ 27 ⤝

To soothe yourself, **LISTEN TO WATER** mindfully – whether it's the splash of ducks in a local pond, the bubble of a nearby river or stream, the rush of the ocean, or a passing rain shower landing on your umbrella.

⤞ 28 ⤝

WATCH THE SUNRISE at the beach – take a comfy chair or a towel, along with a picnic breakfast, and bathe in the glow of a new day.

29

Go on a **TREASURE HUNT**. Invest in a metal detector and head to the beach or a local meadow to scan the ground for hidden riches. Who knows? You might find some long-lost gold.

30

GEOCACHES are hidden outdoor containers filled with trinkets. To start, download the free GPS app and follow the instructions; there are around 3 million caches around the world. When you find a cache, you can take something out but you must replace it with something else of the same or greater value.

⇒⟶ **31** ⟵⇐

If you have an outdoor space, **PLANT FLOWERS** that
bees will love, then enjoy watching them. Keep a log
of the different types of bee that visit. Did you know
that globally there are 20,000 different species?

⇒⟶ **32** ⟵⇐

CLIMB A GRASSY HILL and take in the view. Then
(if it's safe to do so) roll back down to the bottom!

⇒⟶ **33** ⟵⇐

GATHER EYE-CATCHING PEBBLES when you're at
the beach and make a display of your favourites.
Try your hand at making pictures or words and
take a photograph to remember them by.

⤻ 34 ⤺

TRY A NEW ROUTE OR SHORTCUT that you've always wanted to explore. Alternatively, take a different turning on a usual route and enjoy discovering where it leads you.

⤻ 35 ⤺

NORDIC WALKING – walking with poles – began in Finland as a training exercise for cross-country skiers, but it is now a popular whole-body workout that many people enjoy. It can improve your posture and burn up to 46 per cent more calories than normal walking.

⤻ 36 ⤺

Volunteer to help **FEED THE ANIMALS** at a local wildlife park. Some places also offer "meet the animal" experiences so you can get really close to your favourites.

→ 37 ←

Find a QUIET SPOT in the local park and settle
down with a notebook and a pen for some mindful
listening. Concentrate on the sounds around
you and write down everything you can hear.

→ 38 ←

A NIGHT HIKE can be a new way to take in your
surroundings. Set off at dusk. As night falls,
listen to the changes in the sounds around you
and feel the difference in the air. It's advisable
to walk a familiar route so you don't worry
about getting lost, and you should always
take a torch and a fully-charged phone.

39

OUTDOOR BOOTCAMPS are a wonderful way to boost your energy levels. These usually take place in small groups so you'll have plenty of space around you for those jumping jacks.

40

Pass an enjoyable afternoon **FORAGING** for natural ingredients. You can forage for anything from sweet chestnuts, to herbs and berries, to wild garlic.

41

If you're a first-time forager, go with someone who is more experienced, or take a field guidebook, to ensure you *don't pick anything inedible*. Avoid hedgerows along roads, don't deprive wildlife by taking too much from one area and always obtain permission from the landowner.

BUILD A

SANDCASTLE.

⇒→ 43 ←⇐

Go **MAGNET FISHING** for hidden treasure.
Attach a strong magnet to a piece of rope and
"fish" in a pond or lake to see what you can
find. Take a pair of protective gloves and ask
permission if you are on private land.

⇒→ 44 ←⇐

Hold a **MINI FESTIVAL** in your own
back garden. Hang bunting, put up a tent
(or make your own teepee), play your favourite
tunes and soak up the festival atmosphere
from the comfort of your very own home.

⇒→ 45 ←⇐

FEED THE DUCKS at the local pond or the
birds in the park. You don't usually need
to go very far to interact with nature.

⊷⟶ **46** ⟵⊶

Dangling from a rope may not be everyone's idea of a good time, but if you have a head for heights, then **ABSEILING** could be for you. This is the opposite of rock climbing and involves a controlled descent down a vertical face (like a cliff or a tall building) using a rope.

47

Look for a local *climbing centre* and enquire about some lessons, as abseiling is not something to attempt without proper training and supervision. It's also a good idea to start small and work your way up to higher descents.

48

A **WELLNESS RETREAT** is a soothing way to recharge your mind and body. Activities include relaxing pursuits such as yoga, meditation and outdoor swimming.

49

Hang a simple **BIRD FEEDER** in your garden to attract your local feathered friends. If you watch regularly enough, you might get to know your visitors! This is an easy way to witness the beauty of nature without disturbing the balance.

50

If you're a daredevil at heart, investigate free running – or **PARKOUR** – which involves using the world around you as an obstacle course. To be inspired, take a look at videos online. However, to do this safely, look into some lessons first.

– 51 –

Hire

A CANAL BOAT

AND CRUISE THE WATERWAYS.

52

Learn to identify **BIRDSONG**. Find a quiet spot in woodland or a park, settle down with a notepad and pen, and write down how many types you can hear.

53

Record the sounds of the great outdoors on your phone. Do this regularly and build up your collection of **NATURE RECORDINGS**; use the gentle sounds to soothe yourself before bed.

54

On a warm night, **SLEEP OUT UNDER THE STARS** in your garden. If you don't have a garden, why not stay in one belonging to a friend or neighbour? Check to make sure it'll be dry all night and take a sleeping bag and extra blanket in case the temperature drops.

⇒→ **55** ←⇐

If you're an aspiring carpenter, try learning the traditional craft of **WHITTLING**. The best forest woods to look for are fir, pine, cedar, larch and spruce. Look online for advice on whittling for beginners. It goes without saying that you should always take care with any activity involving sharp knives.

⇒→ **56** ←⇐

Set up a **WILDLIFE CAMERA** in your outside space and capture any nocturnal visitors. You'll be surprised at the abundance of activity that goes on while you're asleep.

⇒ 57 ⇐

Visit a local PICK-YOUR-OWN FARM and harvest
some beautiful, juicy, organic berries. They'll
taste amazing compared to the supermarket-
bought varieties, and they won't have
travelled miles to get to your plate.

⇒ 58 ⇐

You don't have to live in a snowy part of the
world to enjoy the thrill of SKIING   instead
you can learn to ski on an outdoor dry slope;
all the fun, but without the wet landing.

⇒ 59 ⇐

Download an app to help you IDENTIFY PLANTS
AND FLOWERS when you are out and about.
Keep a diary of all the things you've seen
and you'll be a nature expert in no time.

☞→ 60 ←☜

Head to an open space in your lunch hour
and **EAT AL FRESCO** with the backdrop of
nature. Take an umbrella and something to
sit on if there's a chance of a shower.

☞→ 61 ←☜

Those with a sense of adventure should try
WINDSURFING. All you need is a wetsuit, a board
and sail, a body of water – and a blustery day.
Begin with a bigger board and a small sail and
have some lessons to pick up the basics.

☞→ 62 ←☜

A **DOWNPOUR** after days of sunshine in summer is
always a welcome relief. The gentle scent of rain on
hot earth cannot be beaten. Get outside and enjoy it.

- 63 -

MAKE A

DAISY

chain.

64

A dragon boat is like a long canoe, about
40 feet (12 metres) long, crewed by a team and
a drummer. Have a look online to see if there is
a club near you. If you'd prefer to watch, look for
a DRAGON BOAT FESTIVAL; it's a thrilling spectacle.

65

Many farms and smallholdings allow visitors
for LAMBING days. These are an adorable way
to get up close with the beauty of nature and
a wonderful experience for animal lovers.

➼→ **66** ←⇇

Go for a walk in autumn. Feel the **CRUNCH OF THE FALLEN LEAVES** underneath your feet and note the new crispness in the air.

➼→ **67** ←⇇

Choose a book with a **WILDERNESS** theme and take it to the local forest or park to read. You'll feel as though you've been transported into the pages.

➼→ **68** ←⇇

GROW YOUR OWN fruit, vegetables or herbs. You can either look into a local allotment space, or simply sow some seeds in a window box. Now only does home-grown produce taste amazing, but you have the satisfaction of knowing your care and attention brought the food into being.

69

Take one photograph of your **FAVOURITE OUTDOOR SPACE** every day. At the end of the year, scroll through your pictures to enjoy the changing seasons all over again.

70

PRACTISE YOUR AIM at an outdoor par 3 golf course. Even future Masters winners have to start somewhere!

71

BE A TOURIST in your own area and look at where you live through fresh eyes. Go to the museum you've always walked past or visit the place you've only ever heard about. You could discover some hidden gems.

⇒→ 72 ←⇐

Dinosaurs roamed all parts of the Earth millions of years ago, so there are a multitude of places ripe for **FOSSIL HUNTING**. Research the best spots in your area and give it a go. The most impressive specimens can often take a long time to find, but the rewards are worth it.

⇒→ 73 ←⇐

Hold a **SUMMER SOLSTICE PARTY**. Cook sumptuous barbecue food, make crowns out of found materials such as flowers, leaves and twigs, play tranquil music and relish the warmth and sunset of the longest day.

74

If you're interested in understanding your surroundings rather than just passing through, look for a guided **NATURE WALK** and hear from an expert as you go.

75

SNORKELLING is a great way to see a whole new world under the water, from stunning shells and coral to beautiful marine life.

76

To snorkel, *you'll need* a mask and some flippers and, if the water is cooler, a wetsuit to keep warm. If you stay in shallow water and are with someone who can swim, you don't need to be a strong swimmer.

– 77 –

Learn to be

AN EXPERT

MINIBEAST HUNTER.

78

Keep an eye on weather websites for details about **ASTRONOMICAL EVENTS**. From supermoons to meteor showers, there is so much to see if we know where – and when – to look.

79

Aim to get outside at least once every day and take a simple photo of your surroundings, something that catches your eye, or the person you're with. Keep all your memories in an **ONLINE ALBUM**.

80

A relaxing way to enjoy being on the water is stand-up **PADDLE BOARDING**, which is usually done at a slow speed in calm water. A few tips: always wear a life jacket, go with someone else and don't paddle after dark.

81

Sunshine and showers? Go **RAINBOW HUNTING**.
All you need is the sun behind you and the
rainstorm ahead of you. Rainbows are easier to
find in seasons where the sun is at a lower angle;
the lower the sun, the more of the rainbow is visible.

82

Go to the forest and make your own **DEN**. Connect
pieces of cane in a tent shape, then tie together a
criss-cross of twigs and small branches across the
frame using natural or organic yarn; keep adding
them until you have sufficient cover. Add a comfy
cushion for a peaceful outdoor reading space.

☞→ **83** ←☜

Get to know your bulbs. Planning ahead and
PLANTING in the cooler months will reward you with
plenty of colourful displays the following year.

☞→ **84** ←☜

COLLECT BERRIES from hedgerows and make
your own liqueur or delicious homemade
jam – then enjoy the fruits of your labour.
Take a field guidebook and avoid any
berries that you aren't familiar with.

☞→ **85** ←☜

Settle down in a meadow and try your hand at
SKETCHING LANDSCAPES. A good art shop can advise
on the best kit for beginners, but all you really need
is a piece of paper and something to draw with!

86

Go POND DIPPING and see what creatures you can find; you simply need a net and an empty jam jar. Once you've enjoyed looking at your finds, and perhaps taken some photos, return them to the water and send them on their way.

87

If you have the space and the time, CHICKENS make lovely outdoor pets – and you'll never be short of fresh eggs.

88

Go BIRDWATCHING. Do some research into your native bird species, where they live and what they eat, and then see how many you can spot. Write a log and take photographs to keep track.

89

Construct a homemade **BUTTERFLY FEEDING STATION** and hang it in a tree or on a balcony. You can use an old glass jar, jug or glass dish. Fill your container with sugar water and watch these beautiful pollinators enjoy the buffet.

90

Try **ZIP WIRES** for a safe but fun-filled adrenaline hit. There are giant zip wires that allow you to whizz through treetops, or you can find smaller-scale versions in some children's play areas (because who says kids have to have all the fun?).

91

Organize an **OUTDOOR SCAVENGER HUNT**!
Make a list of twenty items to find, then
arrange a meeting spot and challenge your
friends to see who finds them first.

92

HIKING, RAMBLING OR FELL-WALKING is a great
– and inexpensive – way to make the most
of your surroundings and enjoy the view.

93

To enjoy a hike in the countryside, *you'll need*
a sturdy pair of waterproof walking boots and a
backpack for your supplies. It's a good idea to
"break in" new boots on a few short walks first.
Always take a phone, plenty of water and a first-aid
kit – and tell someone when you expect to be back.

- 94 -

Go for a

WALK

IN THE SNOW.

DRONES are a great way to practise your flying skills while remaining safely on the ground. Some of them offer amazing photographic opportunities too.

96

In most countries you'll need to register to *fly a drone* and, in some cases, you must also take a theory test. Always make sure you have plenty of space to fly a drone and never fly it near crowds, an airfield or an airport.

If you're out for an autumn walk, collect some dry leaves, take them home and try your hand at **LEAF RUBBINGS**. Place a piece of paper over a leaf and rub the paper with a crayon to reveal the leaf's shape.

98

Have a BARBECUE ON THE BEACH. Toast bread or marshmallows, cook hot dogs, or pack some chairs, a camping table and crockery and enjoy a complete meal. Any food that's cooked and eaten outdoors always seems to taste extra special.

99

Before setting up your barbecue, make sure they are allowed in the area you're planning to visit. If you're cooking meat, always check it's completely cooked through. Most importantly, make sure you take all food leftovers and rubbish with you when you leave.

⇒→ 100 ←⇐

Get in the saddle and try **HORSE RIDING OR PONY TREKKING**. You don't need to own a horse; you can arrange a trip out through a riding stables in your area or take a pony trekking short break.

⇒→ 101 ←⇐

Head to a local **BEAUTY SPOT** and watch the sunset. Take a picnic and witness the magnificent end to the day. Listen out for the new creatures that awaken at dusk.

⇒→ 102 ←⇐

Spend an afternoon **ORIENTEERING**. This activity flexes your navigation skills and all you need is a map and a compass (not your phone's GPS!). You can also compete in events against other people to see who reaches a set point first.

103

If it's a wild water experience you're after, then **LEARN TO SURF**. It's a complex sport to learn, but once you catch your first wave, there'll be no going back.

104

BODYBOARDING is a slightly tamer and less demanding alternative to surfing. Rather than standing on the board, you lie facing forward and paddle. The boards are also lighter to carry.

105

You need to be a *strong swimmer* if you're going to attempt either of these activities. Lessons for both are also vital and instructors will be able to advise you on the correct boards to buy or borrow.

ᐅ→ 106 ←ᐊ

Use odds and ends such as moss, wood, old tiles and straw to build a **BUG HOTEL** and welcome creatures into your garden. Instructions and fresh inspiration can be found online. Why not get creative with it?

ᐅ→ 107 ←ᐊ

Take part in an organized **LITTER PICK** in your local park – or just do your own. Your actions will help to create better surroundings for yourself and others. Make sure to use protective gloves to pick up the litter.

⊱→ 108 ←⊰

You never forget how to **RIDE A BIKE**. Relive
that childhood feeling of the wind in your
face as you use pedal power. (And remember,
you're also never too old to learn.)

⊱→ 109 ←⊰

Whether you ride solo in the forest or in an off-
road competition, **MOUNTAIN BIKING** is a next step
for a confident cyclist with a taste for adventure.
Mountain bikes have sturdier frames and thicker
tyres for better grip. Go on, get muddy!

110

With any kind of cycling, *always wear a cycle
helmet* and make sure you have your bike serviced
regularly. If you're cycling at night, be visible: wear
reflective clothing and fit lights to your bike.

— 111 —

Practise your

BALANCE

ON A SLACKLINE.

⇒⟶ 112 ⟵⇐

If you like a challenge, then **ZORBING**
(also called globe-riding) – where you're
sent down a slope in a large transparent orb –
could be just the sport you're looking for.
Aqua zorbing can also be done on water.

⇒⟶ 113 ⟵⇐

For a bigger adventure, head for the pistes and
LEARN TO SKI. Then chill out and enjoy the
après-ski after an energetic day on the slopes.
Remember to always learn with an expert
and listen to safety instructions carefully.

⇒⟶ 114 ⟵⇐

Volunteer to become a **FRUIT AND VEGETABLE
PICKER**. Many local producers could be
looking for extra pairs of hands.

⇒→ 115 ←⇐

When most of us are sleeping, wildlife is still active. If you're a night owl, sit out on a warm evening and you might catch a glimpse of a local **BADGER OR HEDGEHOG** searching for a snack.

⇒→ 116 ←⇐

SKATEBOARDING offers you the chance to practise your balancing skills – and could give you an alternative eco-friendly way to travel! Invest in a good set of elbow and knee pads, along with a helmet, and learn the basics on a flat surface first before heading to the skate park.

PARASAILING – or parascending – offers all the fun and excitement of a parachute jump, without the leap from a plane. In this activity, you are towed along by a boat in open water, while wearing a harness and a special parachute. As the boat gets faster, up you go!

118

Any *water-based sporting activity* is best booked through an approved provider. This ensures your health and wellbeing is put first, leaving you to enjoy the thrill of the ride.

Nine holes or 18? **GOLF** is another excellent way to get out in the fresh air and enjoy all nature has to offer, while providing exercise and companionship at the same time.

120

ANGLING is a more laid-back outdoor activity. You'll need a good pair of waders, and a tackle shop can help with the right equipment and advice. Listen to the gentle lapping of the water and wait for a bite.

121

NIGHT FISHING can add a touch of excitement to angling. Take some form of shelter with you, remember to wear warm clothing and set up your lighting before it gets dark.

122

To *fish ethically*, you should have a licence. Some areas have limits on the number of fish you can take so do your research first. Above all, focus on the fun and experience, rather than the size of your catch.

⇒ → **123** ← ⇐

Practise your aim in a safe environment with
a spot of **CLAY PIGEON** (or clay target) shooting.
This sport started in around 1875 and involves using
a shotgun to hit fast-moving, flying clay targets.

124

No special equipment or clothing is needed to
give this sport a try. You'll just need to contact a
shooting ground in your area. Qualified instructors
will be on hand to show you what to do.

⊱— 125 —⊰

CAVING is a fascinating way to explore Earth's hidden beauty. Look up cave exploration sites near you to get started!

126

Never enter a cave unless you are with a guide. Take warm clothing – even if it's warm outside, a cave will likely be cool and damp. *Tunnels and passages* can be narrow, so you'll need to be comfortable with small spaces too.

⊱— 127 —⊰

If you're a gamer, there are a host of **AUGMENTED REALITY APPS** for your phone that allow you to play outdoors. Some of the apps simply encourage you to walk – or you could hunt your local parks and gardens for ghosts, or even outrun zombies!

– 128 –

BATHE IN A

NATURAL

hot spring.

129

TENNIS is a sport for all ages, and it's a wonderful way to get out in the fresh air. Find a local court and a partner, and away you go.

130

Next time you're wandering in the great outdoors, find a **SMALL MEMENTO** to remind you of your connection to the natural world. Perhaps you could take a smooth pebble to hold in your pocket, a feather, or a leaf to be pressed.

131

Action-packed **KITESURFING** combines elements of snowboarding, windsurfing and parasailing. In this sport, you are pulled along by a kite and control your direction using a board so that you can ride over the waves like a snowboarder.

➤ **132** ⬅

If you're a real daredevil, then hone your stunt skills with a **WING-WALKING** experience. You'll certainly need a taste for adventure, but the exhilaration and excitement will make this something to remember.

133

You'll need warm, comfortable clothing and flat shoes – wing-walking organizers will usually provide you with overalls to go over your clothes and goggles to cover any glasses. You'll need to be physically fit enough to climb up onto the roof of a bi-plane, and certain medical conditions could rule out this activity.

A lovely seaside activity is **CRABBING**. This involves lowering bait into the water, attached to a line with a weight. Once the crab takes hold you can lift the line slowly and observe these captivating creatures before returning them to the ocean.

135

For *successful crabbing*, you'll need a line, a large bucket (half-filled with seawater), a net and some bait, such as bacon or sardines. Don't put too many crabs in the bucket at once and keep fingers away from their pincers!

WILDLIFE WATCHING in your local park can be a satisfying way to spend an afternoon. Settle down and see how many different kinds of life you can see.

SCUBA DIVING involves using tanks of oxygen and breathing equipment to travel deep under the sea. You'll be able to spot many ocean dwellers such as turtles, larger fish and beautiful corals as well as feeling humbled by the expanse of water that surrounds you.

138

If you're interested in learning to scuba dive, *search online* for an instructor to learn the skills you will need. When you are able to go out, always dive with a buddy, watch your air level and know your limits. It's important not to touch anything; the idea of scuba diving is to observe the beauty of the ocean.

➣→ 139 ←➣

Learning about **ANIMAL TRACKS** can be an
enjoyable way to investigate species in your area.
Leave a large tray of wet sand in your garden
overnight and then see if you can identify
any footprints the following morning.

➣→ 140 ←➣

One exhilarating winter sport to try is
SNOWBOARDING. As with any new sport, advice
from an expert and proper beginners' lessons
are an imperative before you hit the slopes.

➣→ 141 ←➣

Next time you're at the beach, spot native **SEABIRDS**.
Sometimes we can be so focused on the ocean itself,
that we forget to look up at the cliffs and the sky.

MOUNTAINEERING is the sport of climbing mountains, and it can offer a personal challenge unlike any other. There are a wide range of different types of terrain to focus on, from granite and rock to ice-covered glaciers.

143

Before setting foot on a mountain, *you need to be physically fit*. Running and cycling will increase cardiovascular fitness and upper body strength. You'll need to take a course, and map reading, camping and fire-building skills will also be essential knowledge. Mountaineering may require a lot of preparation, but the reward of reaching the summit makes it worth all the effort!

➵➛ 144 ←⟨

Get up close and personal with a **BIRD OF PREY** at a falconry centre or a display and enjoy watching these masters of the sky. If you're feeling brave, you could volunteer to be the landing post!

➵➛ 145 ←⟨

Learn to **PILOT A LIGHT AIRCRAFT**. Look for your nearest flight school and ask about some lessons – then enjoy the fabulous views of the natural world in miniature while you learn a new skill. You could be taking the first step toward earning your pilot's licence.

146

Do your research first to find out if *learning to fly* might be for you – there are lots of magazines and online forums to ask for advice.

148

Practise **YOGA** outside at dawn – feel the fresh air enter your lungs as you salute the sun.

149

Invest in a **CAMPING HAMMOCK** and you'll have a comfortable, ready-made bed as long as you have two trees from which to suspend it. There are plenty of online videos on hammock camping for beginners.

150

ROWING is a great way to get fit and take in the riverside views while you're at it. You can row solo or join a local sailing club to learn the basics.

➤ **151** ⬅

POWER WALKING is an excellent way to build up fitness and cardiovascular health. Start with normal walking, gradually building up your speed. Walk tall and keep one foot on the ground at all times to make sure you're not actually running. Breathe in the cleansing air and swing your arms as you walk.

➤ **152** ⬅

Take a trip on an open-air ferry or paddle boat. **CRUISING DOWN THE RIVER** makes a refreshing change from sitting in a stuffy car or train and you can enjoy the fresh air and sunshine.

153

FORAGE FOR MINT OR NETTLE LEAVES and then make your own tea. There's no mistaking the beautiful and refreshing scent of mint, and nettle tea is earthy and comforting.

154

Make your own mint or nettle tea by **STEEPING THE LEAVES IN BOILING WATER** in a teapot for 4–5 minutes (longer if you want stronger tea). Use around double the amount of water to leaves. Then strain the liquid and sweeten with some honey.

155

If you're foraging for nettles, wear gloves to minimize the chance of being stung. As with any foraging activity, take a guidebook with you to make sure you can *correctly identify the plants*.

156

Tree-top adventure days offer you the chance to **UNLEASH YOUR INNER TARZAN!** High ropes, swings, obstacles, bridges and zip wires are just some examples of the activities in store.

157

When taking part in a *tree-top adventure*, listen to any instructions and wear all of the protective equipment on the day. You'll need comfortable clothing suitable for the weather and flat shoes; you might also want to take your own gloves.

158

Construct a homemade **BIRD FEEDER** to encourage nature to come to you. You could punch holes in old bottles and fill them with seeds. Look up tutorials online for more ideas, then sit out and watch your winged visitors.

159

Why go for a walk in the outdoors when you could ROLLER-SKATE? Feel the freedom as you glide along on your own set of wheels! Once you get the hang of it, you could even learn a few tricks.

160

If you're a novice or it's been a while since you wore wheels, start slowly and get your balance on level ground to begin with. For extra precautions, invest in a helmet, elbow and knee pads and make sure your skates offer good support for your ankles.

161

Visit an **OUTDOOR ICE RINK** for some winter fun. Practise near the edge first, where you can hold on to something, and don't head out to the middle until you're confident you can balance and stop.

162

If you're a **REMOTE-CONTROL ENTHUSIAST**, take your pick from model boats, cars and trains. Build your own from kits, or join a local club where you can get competitive against other vehicles in open space.

163

Netball and basketball have never gone out of style. Grab a friend and **HEAD TO THE COURTS** at your local park or, if you're on your own, practise your long shots from the halfway line.

— 164 —

DIP YOUR

FEET INTO

moving water.

⊱⟶ 165 ⟵⊰

SAILING is an exhilarating day out. There's nothing quite like the freedom of being out on the water. The easiest way to start is to find a sailing school and take it from there.

⊱⟶ 166 ⟵⊰

Invest in a **SKIPPING ROPE** and teach yourself how to skip. All you need is a little coordination and some patience – and the best part is, you can do this anywhere, whether it's the park, at the beach or in a forest.

⊱⟶ 167 ⟵⊰

For a picnic with a difference, head out on a warm night and **EAT UNDER THE STARS**. Charge up some solar lights during the day and take them along to decorate your blanket.

→ 168 ←

RUNNING is one of the easiest ways to reconnect with nature. Run through your local park, along the seafront, or through open country and explore the world around you. There are several apps you can download to get started. You'll need comfy clothes and, if you're going to run regularly, a supportive pair of running shoes. If you are running at night, wear reflective clothing or lights.

→ 169 ←

TRAIL RUNNING is one natural next step for an established runner. Head for the forest and the hills – the muddier, the better! You will need a pair of trail shoes with a good grip.

170

Grab a football and enjoy a KICKABOUT IN THE PARK. If it's just you, try your hand (or foot) at kick-ups. How many can you do without letting the ball drop?

171

FRESHWATER CRAYFISH are another delicacy that you can forage for. The whole crayfish is edible, but the tails are the most widely used in recipes. Make sure to research your country's foraging regulations first though, as some species are endangered.

172

Give grocery shopping an outdoor twist: FARMERS' MARKETS are a great way to source fresh locally grown produce. You'll be buying quality goods and supporting local businesses at the same time.

⊱→ 173 ←⊰

On a hot day, let loose in your garden and host a **WATER-BALLOON FIGHT**. Then lay back in the sunshine to dry off. Don't forget your sun cream.

⊱→ 174 ←⊰

Visit a **MODEL VILLAGE** and admire the detailed handiwork involved in recreating real life in miniature.

⊱→ 175 ←⊰

Becoming a **YOUTH GROUP LEADER** is a brilliant way to get involved and inspire the next generation of outdoor pioneers, as well as learn new skills yourself. Many local groups are often looking for help so check online to see if there's one nearby.

176

If you swim regularly and fancy something
a little different, head out for some invigorating
OPEN-WATER SWIMMING – it will make you feel alive!

177

Open water is much colder than pool water, so stick
to the edges when you first enter in case you need to
get out. If it's your first open-water swim, keep time
spent in the water quite short to begin with and
increase it gradually on subsequent visits. Always
bring lots of warm clothes to put on afterward.
It's best to go swimming with someone else, or
head to an *organized outdoor swim session*. Don't
just jump into the nearest river, lake or ocean.

 **178**

Next time you're at the beach, try **BEACHCOMBING**.
Meander along the coastline and see if you
can find anything attractive or of value:
pieces of sea glass, fossils and unusual stones
can all make lovely collectible art. You
may even find a message in a bottle.

 **179**

Offer to assist a neighbour with their **GARDENING**.
Not everyone is mobile enough to be able to
do this. You'll be enjoying the outdoors and
helping someone out at the same time.

➷ **180** ↢

If you have the room, put a **TRAMPOLINE**
in your garden. Bounce whenever you get
the chance, but don't attempt somersaults
unless you're completely confident!

Photograph your name

IN THE SAND

FOR A LASTING MEMORY.

⊳—→ 182 ←—⊲

SNOW TUBING is an activity that can be enjoyed on winter slopes. This simply involves sliding down a hill in an inflated tube! If you live somewhere with little snow, some dry ski slopes also offer this activity.

⊳—→ 183 ←—⊲

Nothing beats **GOOD OLD-FASHIONED CAMPING** for a taste of the outdoors. Many tents nowadays are the pop-up kind – so no more tangling with tent pegs and ropes!

⊳—→ 184 ←—⊲

If you'd like your outdoor experience to be a little more refined, try **GLAMPING**. This is a more luxurious kind of camping where you sleep in self-contained huts, yurts or teepees.

➤→ **185** ←◀

For a true outdoor experience, try **WILD CAMPING** – pitching your tent outside the boundaries of designated campsites and spending the night in the true wilderness.

186

Different countries have different regulations about wild camping, so *check the rules* for your area before you go, and always seek permission from the landowner. Any kit – tent included – will need to fit inside a rucksack that you are able to carry, so it's advisable to travel light. Finally, remember the most important rule for any type of camping: leave no trace.

➤ 187 ←

If you like your outdoor games, the classic French game of **BOULES** can be played as an evening camping activity. Simply roll the balls (boules) as close to the smaller target ball as you can.

➤ 188 ←

A game of **KUBB** is a great way to bring some friendly competition to your campsite. The game is similar to skittles: wooden blocks are lined up a short distance away and players take turns at trying to hit the targets with a ball.

➤ 189 ←

Get in touch with your inner child and have a **SLEEPING-BAG RACE**. Set a start point and a finish line and huddle into your sleeping bag. On your marks, get set, go!

⤐ 190 ↢⥅

CAPTURE THE FLAG is a traditional camping game where two teams each have a flag secured to a base in their own "territory". The object is to capture the other team's flag and bring it back to your base; opposing team members knock each other out of the game by tagging.

⤐ 191 ↢⥅

NIGHT-TIME HIDE-AND-SEEK adds an extra challenge to a childhood favourite. You could include animal sounds, whereby each person is assigned an animal and must make the sounds to give the seeker a better chance.

⤐ 192 ↢⥅

Try **TORCH TAG**: can you tag your fellow campers with your torch beam? Loser cooks the next morning's breakfast!

193

Get to grips with ROCK CLIMBING and give your
head for heights a true test! This is definitely an
outdoor sport for an adventure hunter. It's all about
balance, footwork, strength and ingenuity as you
work your way toward your choice of summit.

194

Rock climbing is not without its risks, so if you
do decide to go for it, training is key. Look for a
climbing centre and ask about beginners' lessons.
It will also be advantageous to start working on
your core and upper body strength, as this is
what gives you power and control as a climber.

⇒→ 195 ←⇐

To **FEEL AS FREE AS A BIRD**, opt for the next best thing: hang-gliding. In this sport, you are attached to the "wings" of the glider using a harness. Pilots launch by running into the wind from a high point, such as a hill or a cliff, then fly down to the ground using the currents of air. You'll need the willingness to let go and try something extraordinary.

196

To get started with *hang-gliding*, join a club and take lessons. If you want a one-off experience, book a tandem hang-glide, so you are free to enjoy the view.

⤐ 197 ⟵⤙

FORAGE FOR DANDELIONS and do some culinary experiments. Add the leaves to salad or fry them up with other greens as a side dish; the yellow flower heads can be added to bread or pickled. The only part you shouldn't eat are the dandelion seed heads – or "clocks".

198

Remember not to forage for dandelions along public roads where weedkiller may have been used. Stick to *open areas and meadows*.

⤐ 199 ⟵⤙

If you're a good open-water swimmer, consider training to be a **BEACH LIFEGUARD**. Not only will this allow you to spend plenty of time outdoors in the sunshine, but you may also save someone's life.

- 200 -

SEARCH FOR THE

PRETTIEST
SHELLS

on the beach.

201

For a different perspective to your pictures, practise taking **OUTDOOR PHOTOGRAPHS AT NIGHT**. There are some great apps to help you get the best from the camera settings on your phone, or you can experiment with different exposures using an SLR camera.

202

Relive a childhood game and **PLAY CONKERS IN AUTUMN**. Collect the biggest horse chestnuts you can find, make holes in them and thread them onto pieces of string. Then take turns to hit each other's conkers until there are none left.

203

Conker safety: aim carefully and try not to hit your opponent's knuckles with your conker.

204

SKYDIVING – jumping from a plane with a parachute – is the ultimate outdoor adventure to cross off your bucket list. You can take lessons and become qualified to do a solo drop, or you can book a one-off experience and do a tandem jump with an instructor, both of which will get the adrenaline flowing.

205

Of course, you'll need a head for heights to be able to step out of a moving plane. The most important thing is to do your research and *find a reputable provider*. Listen carefully to everything you're told during training – both on the ground and once you're in the air. Then enjoy the ride down!

☞→ 206 ←☜

HATCH BUTTERFLIES FROM CATERPILLARS and release them into the wild. You can buy kits to do this which explain the lifecycle. Watch their daily progress and then let them take flight.

☞→ 207 ←☜

Try to **INCREASE YOUR STEP COUNT** each day by walking further than you normally would. You might spot something new or take in a different view.

☞→ 208 ←☜

Some beach locations offer trips round the harbour or along the coast in a speedboat, or on a banana boat. What better way to **EXPERIENCE THE THRILL OF THE WAVES?**

209

Collect some frogspawn and WATCH TADPOLES GROW into froglets. To prepare, you'll need a large tank with stones in the base filled with pond water or rainwater. You'll also need a net to collect the frogspawn, but don't take too many. Pop them in the tank and observe them over a few months, lowering the water level as they grow so they can breathe.

210

Make sure you *release the froglets* in the same place that you found the frogspawn. In most countries it's fine to collect tadpoles and watch them develop at home, but do check your local laws in case it isn't allowed.

Organize a **TREASURE HUNT** that you have to drive
or cycle around, with hidden clues along the
route. The prize could be as simple as having the
last team member in buy everyone a coffee.

212

If you want to attempt a *driving or cycling treasure
hunt,* choose an area that all participants are familiar
with, and remember not to get so carried away
with the game that you forget about road safety.

If you love **HORSES,** see if any local stables
need a helping hand – it's a great way to
spend time with these noble animals and you
may even get to take one out for a ride.

⇒→ 214 ←⇐

Train for and enter a **HALF MARATHON**. Do it
for a charity, or just for yourself. No matter
how you do it – whether you walk, jog, run or
sprint – you'll feel amazing having completed
it, and over the weeks you will have spent
so much time in the great outdoors.

⇒→ 215 ←⇐

If you have the inclination, why not aim for
a **FULL MARATHON** the next time around? Frame
your finisher's photograph, display it proudly and
remember the achievement every time you look at
it. Marathon routes cover all kinds of terrain, so
wherever you like to run, you can use this challenge
to spend more time in your favourite landscapes.

☞ 216 ☜

Push yourself to the limit and take part in
a muddy **OBSTACLE COURSE** competition.
Training advice is usually available from the
organizer of the event to help you prepare.

☞ 217 ☜

GRASS SURFING is similar to skateboarding,
but you ride on a board with no wheels. Most
riders remove the wheels from a skateboard and
then find a dry grassy slope to "surf" down.

218

With grass surfing, choose a gentle incline to
start with. *Safety-wise*, apply the same rules as
skateboarding: wear a helmet as well as elbow
and knee pads. Check your slope carefully first to
make sure there are no big dips or large rocks.

Enjoy crunching

THROUGH
FALLEN

AUTUMN LEAVES.

220

SWIMMING WITH DOLPHINS is one of the most life-enhancing outdoor activities you can do. Being up close to these wonderful ocean creatures is an encounter you'll never forget.

221

Although dolphins have a reputation for their playful and intelligent nature, they are still wild animals. *Listen to any instructions* you're given and treat them with respect.

222

Right up there with a dolphin swim is **WHALE WATCHING**. Catching a glimpse of these gentle giants in the wild is unforgettable and special. Depending on where you live, you may not have to travel far to experience this. Otherwise, it could be something to add to your bucket list.

223

Channel your inner Robin Hood and have a go at **ARCHERY**. There are two types: target archery (which involves loosing arrows at a stationary board from a set distance) and field archery (which usually means hitting targets from different distances in woodland). Most beginners start with target archery.

224

Kits are available for novices, and it's best to visit a specialist shop for advice, although it's advisable to *attend an archery try-out day or book an experience first*. If you're interested in doing it regularly, you'll need to join a club to practise the sport safely under supervision.

225

Practise **MEDITATION OUTSIDE** and feel the warmth of the sun, the calming breeze or the gentle rain on your skin as your stress melts away. Breathe in and out slowly. Observe your thoughts as they pass through your mind.

226

Pick a weekend where you have nothing planned, **STICK A PIN IN A MAP** and visit wherever it lands. Make it a rule that you have to find something to do outdoors when you get there!

227

Find a local park bench and **PEOPLE-WATCH**. Simply watching the world go by is an amazing way to relax. Take care not to stare at people; you don't want to make them uncomfortable.

>→ 228 ←<

LASER TAG is a fun and different way to spend a weekend, and a great activity to take part in with a group of family and friends. There are countless settings and varieties of gameplay, but "battles" often take place in woodland so it's an innovative way to spend time outdoors. Remember to always wear the protective equipment provided and follow the rules.

>→ 229 ←<

COASTEERING is an adrenaline-filled way to explore the coastline, which involves climbing over rocks and jumping from cliffs. Always arrange this with a trustworthy company.

>→ 230 ←<

Spend an afternoon chilling out in or around some **ANCIENT RUINS**. Take a picnic and imagine times gone by.

231

Next time you're at a rocky beach, BUILD A CAIRN. This a piece of artwork made from stacking stones. See how many you can balance.

232

Remember the golden rule of visiting any natural environment is to *leave no trace*. This means after you've finished stacking stones and rocks, you should return them to where you found them. It's fine to have fun with the activity and take a photo to remember it by, but leaving rocks stacked could pose a risk to wildlife and other visitors.

233

Search out a local abandoned building and
be **INVENTIVE WITH PHOTOGRAPHY**. Take shots
from different angles at different times of
day and appreciate the way that nature has
reclaimed the man-made structure.

234

By abandoned, we don't mean just anywhere that's
been boarded up, particularly as buildings only
tend to be covered when they are unsafe. Instead,
stick to derelict properties that are left open to
the elements and always approach with caution.

235

Visit a **NATIONAL PARK OR GARDEN** on your
next day off. Rain or shine, relax and
soak up the floral atmosphere. Take a
packed lunch and put your feet up.

– 236 –

Let nature

BE YOUR

GO-TO THERAPY.

➤ 237 ←

If you have the space and the funds, invest in an **OUTDOOR HOT TUB**. It'll be a welcome change from spending evenings in front of the TV, even in winter.

➤ 238 ←

Become in tune with the Earth's natural rhythm, and mark the June and December **SOLSTICES,** which are the longest and shortest days in the southern and northern hemispheres. Plant a new tree or simply hug an existing one to celebrate the occasion.

➤ 239 ←

Introduce an abundance of colour in your garden by **PLANTING FLOWERS**. Investigate which blooms will do well in your area and get in touch with your green fingers!

➣—→ **240** ←—❮

On a chilly evening, **LIGHT A BONFIRE** and enjoy the
warmth and company of friends or family. Toast
marshmallows and serve warming beverages.

241

Always *check before you light your fire* to make sure
no animals have hidden underneath. Only burn
natural wood and don't use flammable liquids to
light it; instead use paper and kindling (cardboard
egg boxes work well). Stand well back from the fire
when it's alight and keep a bucket of water nearby
in case of emergencies. Finally, double-check
your fire is completely extinguished at the end
of the evening; glowing embers might reignite.

242

Watch a panorama unfold beneath you in a HELICOPTER RIDE. It's noisier and often more turbulent than a plane, but the incredible aerial views of the natural world below just can't be beaten.

243

Have a barbecue where everyone brings and tries something completely new to eat. You might discover your NEW FAVOURITE DISH.

244

For some simple summer fun, make a SLIP 'N' SLIDE in your garden. You can make one from a large tarpaulin – just add some skin-friendly soap and a hose. Take the slide one person at a time and be careful not to crash into anything at the end!

245

Add a touch of fun to your next road trip by turning off the satnav and using a **PAPER MAP**. This might work better when you have a little more time on your hands!

246

Participate in a **BEACH CLEAN-UP**. It doesn't have to be an organized event; simply taking the time yourself to clear some of the beach debris will make a contribution and help keep the environment safe for both humans and precious marine life.

247

Experience how the first aeronauts must have felt and ascend to the great blue yonder in a **HOT-AIR BALLOON RIDE**. Enjoy the fresh, clean air as you float above the hustle and bustle.

⊷→ **248** ←⊷

Don't let the outdoor fun stop when the temperature
drops; **CAMPING IN THE COLDER MONTHS** can still
be enjoyable. Play games and explore – you'll
probably appreciate the warmth of a fire more, too.

249

Make sure your tent and sleeping bag are the right
size for you – extra space means it'll take longer
for the air to warm around you – and place layers
underneath your sleeping bag as well as on top.
Dress warmly to sleep: wear socks and, if it's
particularly cold, gloves. A hat will stop body heat
being lost through the top of your head. Cover any
equipment that's likely to frost up overnight.

A tour of a **VINEYARD** in the sunshine is a lovely, relaxing way to spend an afternoon. You can even sample the wares.

251

Always call ahead to book a tour of a vineyard. It goes without saying that you shouldn't drive yourself home after wine-tasting; make sure you *designate a driver*.

SPARKLERS might be associated with bonfire night, but they can bring a sense of celebration to your campfire or outdoor gathering at any time of year! Take a small bucket with you to drop used sparklers into and then safely dispose of them.

- 253 -

WALK

BAREFOOT

ALONG THE BEACH.

254

Don't confine yourself to a gym; many parks now have **OUTDOOR FITNESS EQUIPMENT**. Take care to wipe it down before and after you use it, so it's clean for you and shows consideration for other users.

255

The traditional craft of **BUILDING A RAFT** is a good way to put woodwork and knotting skills to good use. The idea is to tie items such as barrels, pallets and wood together with strong rope so that it's buoyant enough to keep you afloat.

256

It's best to try out your raft on a calm body of water, like a lake or quiet stream. As with any water-based activity, always *wear a lifejacket*.

➣➝ **257** ⭠⭠⭠

Walk in the woods and **HUG A TREE**. Close your
eyes, breathe deeply and feel its calming energy
flow through your body. Feel humbled by the
tree's age and by the many generations of wildlife
that could have sheltered in its canopy.

➣➝ **258** ⭠⭠⭠

Embrace the simple joy that comes from spending
time in the sea, and **JUMP IN THE WAVES**. Wade into
the shallows and try to jump over them as they
crash onto the shore, or go in deeper and feel the
water carrying you back as each wave passes you.

➤ **259** ←

Go **LLAMA OR ALPACA TREKKING**. Look up farms near you where you can help the handlers take these gentle, inquisitive animals on their daily walk.

➤ **260** ←

Write down ten **LOCAL, RURAL LOCATIONS** you've never been to and set yourself the challenge of visiting them all within a certain timeframe. This is a great way to make sure that you actually follow through on the things you've said you'd do "one day".

➤ **261** ←

Keep camping eco-friendly by going **CARBON NEUTRAL**. Things to try include: eating only locally grown food, using solar-powered torches and lights, and avoiding single-use plastics.

262

COOK SOMETHING DIFFERENT on your campfire: try corn on the cob or pineapple chunks on skewers. Bananas cut through the centre and sprinkled with chocolate and marshmallows also taste amazing. Wrap them in foil and leave in the coals for around ten minutes.

263

If you're camping with other people, challenge everyone to tell a **CREEPY STORY** around the campfire. Give them warning so they can plan in advance. How spooky can you be?

264

CLASSIC PARTY GAMES aren't just for parties; you can play "musical camp chairs" instead. Make sure to do this away from your campfire or cooking stove in case anyone trips while running for a seat!

265

When the sun has fully risen, insert a tall stick in the ground in full sunlight. Note where the shadow falls, wait for the next full hour and then place a rock with that digit painted on it at that point – for example, if it's 7 a.m., place the "7" rock in line with the shadow. Return every hour until you reach 6 p.m. and you'll have a SUNDIAL.

266

Hire an ELECTRIC BIKE for your next countryside adventure. A bike allows you to cover a greater distance, and an electric one makes hills less of a strain so it's easier for you to sit back and enjoy the world passing by.

⇒→ 267 ←⇐

Take an old length of rope and place a marker in the middle, then have an old-fashioned tug of war. This makes a **GREAT CAMPING ACTIVITY**.

268

For *tug of war*, only hold the rope with your hands. Tying it around your waist or other parts of your body could result in injury. If the rope is rough, wear a pair of gloves.

⇒→ 269 ←⇐

Plant **SEED BOMBS** in your garden or a public space. They will grow into a stunning wildflower meadow that bees will love. You can make your own by mixing flower seeds with powdered clay and compost and squeezing it all together.

Study

LEAVES

TO IDENTIFY TREES.

⤖ 271 ⬿

Try your hand at writing a **POEM ABOUT NATURE**. Find a quiet spot somewhere peaceful and settle down with a pen and paper. Write down your thoughts as you absorb the sounds around you. Keep your poems just for yourself, or share them with a loved one.

⤖ 272 ⬿

MAKE A BOAT out of natural materials that you find on the ground. Check the forest floor for large leaves which could act as sails and some sturdy twigs to make a raft or a mast.

⤖ 273 ⬿

Build up your skills at **STONE-SKIMMING**. All you need is a large body of water and some flat stones (make sure there is nobody in front of you as you throw).

▷→ **274** ←◁

Try a variation on traditional **I SPY** with a coastal alphabet hunt. Take a stroll and look for things that begin with each letter. Anchor, beach, crab…

▷→ **275** ←◁

Attempt to navigate through a **MAZE**. Find your way to the middle as a group or race your friends and family to see who can find their way the fastest – both in and back out! You could even celebrate reaching the centre with a flask of tea or coffee and a slice of cake.

⇒→ 276 ←⇐

Spend an afternoon in the countryside and make your own **SHORT FILM** using the camera on your phone. There are many apps that can help you put together a professional-looking end product.

⇒→ 277 ←⇐

You don't need a large outdoor space to grow plants. Colourful old wellies, boots or tins on a balcony or windowsill make great **PLANTERS**. You can drill holes in the bottom to let water drain through.

⇒→ 278 ←⇐

CRAB FOOTBALL is a tried-and-tested camping game. First, set up two goals, then lean back on your hands and push up with your feet into a "crab" position. Kick the ball toward your team's goal!

⇒→ 279 ←⇐

A **NEW MOON** symbolizes a fresh start, so harness its power by hosting a celebratory party. Create a calming space outdoors, place healing crystals in a circle, then sit in the centre and write down your dreams.

⊃ ▸ 280 ←⇐

If you're an **ANIMAL LOVER**, consider adopting a dog; they will need a walk every day. Alternatively, you could keep pet rabbits in the garden. Both will allow you to spend more time outside.

281

Work with your neighbours and turn an old piece of disused public land into a **COMMUNITY GARDEN**. If you're arty, you could bring joy to an empty wall and organize a mural painting project.

282

Go via the proper routes to ask whoever owns the land or the wall if you can adopt it. If you can't find out, place a notice near the site explaining what you would like to do. Hopefully the message will reach the right person to *get your project started*.

283

ASK LOCAL BUSINESSES AND VOLUNTEERS
if they would be happy to donate time and equipment – such as plants, seeds or paint.

– 284 –

MAKE A

SNOW
SCULPTURE

in your garden.

⊱→ 285 ←⊰

If you love running then **FELL-RUNNING** could be your next challenge. It involves running over extreme and rugged terrain, and you'll also need navigation skills as routes are often unmarked. Dress appropriately and wear sturdy running shoes.

⊱→ 286 ←⊰

CONTAINER VEGETABLE GARDENING on a balcony or windowsill can be very productive. Produce such as lettuce, tomatoes and herbs can all easily be grown in tubs and pots.

⊱→ 287 ←⊰

Hold a **WINTER SOLSTICE PARTY.** Make lanterns, garland a yule tree with natural decorations, craft pomanders and pass the darkest night of the year by candlelight in the company of friends.

288

CROSS-COUNTRY SKIING is an extreme winter sport for the more adventurous. You'll need leg strength and stamina to propel yourself forward, and you can take in the stunning alpine views at the same time.

289

Cross-country skis are lighter in weight than traditional skis – this means they can take some getting used to, even for a seasoned skier. *If you are starting out,* stick to the well used routes until you become acclimatized to the new technique.

290

Take a break with a difference and stay on a **WORKING FARM**. Be prepared for early starts and long days.

291

Many local wildlife organizations co-ordinate **WILDLIFE SURVEYS** – from butterfly, bug and amphibian counts, to recording the number of local bird species. Get involved!

292

Pick up **FRESHLY FALLEN FLOWERS** and press them in tissue paper within the pages of a book. Then put all your favourites in a special album or use them for crafting.

293

BEEKEEPING is a hobby with a difference. Observing and caring for these amazing insects will give an insight into their busy and endangered world.

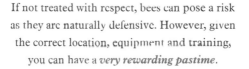

294

If not treated with respect, bees can pose a risk as they are naturally defensive. However, given the correct location, equipment and training, you can have a *very rewarding pastime*.

295

To keep bees, you will need some space, and you should ask your neighbours if they are comfortable with you doing so. Bees can travel quite far for pollen, so if someone locally has an allergy or expresses concern, look into a **BEEKEEPING CLUB** instead.

296

If you want to awaken to the first rays of the sun, uninterrupted, then **BIVOUACKING** – camping with no tent – offers a true back-to-nature experience. A "bivvy" is a breathable bag that wraps around your sleeping bag to protect you from the elements.

297

Though bivvying can be a little uncomfortable, with the right equipment you'll have a good night's rest. As well as your bivvy bag, *you'll need* a sleeping bag and mat, a warm hat and gloves, plenty of food and water, and a waterproof breathable jacket. A bag to keep your belongings dry overnight is also essential.

– 298 –

SIT

IN THE PARK

and just listen.

➤ **299** ⬅

Volunteer as a **DOG-WALKER** and enjoy time in the outdoors with some new four-legged friends.

➤ **300** ⬅

If you enjoy running, consider joining a **CROSS-COUNTRY RUNNING CLUB** to have a chance to explore new places and terrains and meet new people at the same time.

➤ **301** ⬅

Collect fallen apples in your local area and **BAKE AN APPLE PIE**. Try not to pick fruit from trees on private property, but if they have dropped to the ground on public land then help yourself.

 **302**

WALK TO WORK rather than relying on the bus or train. Wear comfortable shoes or trainers and take your office shoes in a bag to change into when you arrive. Enjoy the breeze and the sunshine, rather than breathe stuffy recycled air.

303

If walking the whole route is a step too far, try *hopping off the bus* two or three stops earlier than you normally would on the way to work. On the way home, walk back to that stop before you catch the bus again.

304

For an adrenaline-charged trip out on the waves,
HIRE A JET SKI. Different sizes are available – for
either a single rider, or two or three people.

305

Always *wear water-safety equipment* when
operating a jet ski and stick to the speed limit.
Jet ski etiquette for your area – for example,
rights of way and observing other vessels – may
be advertized locally. If not, do some research.

306

SNOWSHOEING involves wearing large flat
footwear to walk over thick snow. This sport
allows you to enjoy solitude and precious
thinking time on hiking trails that could be
crowded and noisy at other times of year.

307

Combine exercise, leisure and enjoyment of your surroundings, by going on a **PUB WALK**. Plan your route in advance to decide where you'll stop and which route to take. It might be wise to cap how long you stay in every establishment, with a one-drink limit at each.

308

Organize a regular **CHARITY CAR-WASH EVENT**. Have neighbours and friends sponsor you to wash their vehicles and then donate your takings to a worthy cause. This can be a fun way to spend time outside with friends, while doing a good deed at the same time.

⇒→ 309 ←⇐

Visit one of the most picturesque sights the Earth has to offer: a **WATERFALL**. Admire the cascading water and feel at one with nature.

⇒→ 310 ←⇐

Find some **COLOURFUL CHALK** and get creative on a footpath. Doodle away to your heart's content – it will wash away with the next downpour, so you can do it again.

⇒→ 311 ←⇐

If you can throw accurately then **DISC GOLF** could be for you. The rules are similar to traditional golf, in that it takes place over nine or 18 holes, but instead of hitting a ball, it involves throwing a disc toward a target with a basket.

➥→ 312 ←↢

Practise identifying different types of wood when you're out and about to become a **CAMPFIRE MASTER**. The best campfires are built with specific kinds of dry wood. Ash, for example, burns at a steady rate so your fire will last longer. Softer woods such as cedar and pine will burn fast, but you'll need to keep adding to your fire to keep it going.

➥→ 313 ←↢

Fill a clean glass container with alternating layers of sand and soil, add some worms and some vegetable peelings. Drill some holes in the lid of the jar and you have your own **WORM RECYCLING CENTRE**. Watch them at work as they break down your food waste.

314

Save energy and harness the power of the sun to make your own **SUN TEA**. Place eight teabags inside a glass container filled with 1 gallon (4 litres) of water, and leave it to brew in the sunshine for around 5 hours. Keep an eye on it through the day. The water will heat gently and voila: sun tea.

315

Go **PUMPKIN PICKING**! With your harvest, you can make pumpkin pie or soup, roast the seeds to liven up a salad and then use the outer skin to carve for decorations.

316

Spend an evening at an **OUTDOOR CINEMA**. These venues are gaining popularity, and the good old-fashioned drive-in is enjoying a revival too.

– 317 –

Build a

DEN

IN THE WOODS.

⤳ **318** ⬱

Make snow ice cream for a **WINTER TREAT**. Mix together evaporated milk, sugar and vanilla essence to taste, then head out and collect 8–10 cups of freshly fallen snow. Gradually mix in your milk mixture and stir to ice-cream consistency – not too slowly, or it will melt. Wrap up warm and eat it outside.

319

Make sure to only use really fresh snow for *snow ice cream*. Once it's been there overnight, it's not going to be clean enough to eat.

320

FORAGING needn't stop when the weather turns cooler. There are all kind of treats to be found, including blackberries and sloe berries, crab apples, hazelnuts and beech nuts.

321

When foraging, always take a guidebook and make sure you *know what you are picking*. As mentioned earlier in this book, try to avoid picking fruit from hedgerows close to roads as they may have absorbed exhaust fumes and been sprayed with pesticides.

322

Play **NATURE BINGO**! Draw up some bingo cards with names of animals and objects – laminate them if you like. Then go on a nature walk and see who can fill their card first.

⤜→ **323** ←⤛

If you are a keen swimmer, look for an **OUTDOOR LIDO OR SWIMMING POOL**. Doing lengths of breaststroke, butterfly or front crawl in the elements adds an extra layer of invigoration.

⤜→ **324** ←⤛

LIE IN THE SUN and listen to music. Put on a classical recording and absorb each note as you feel the warm rays on your body.

⤜→ **325** ←⤛

Hop in the car, roll down the windows and take a drive. Have no particular destination in mind and **SEE WHERE THE ROAD TAKES YOU.**

- 326 -

SEARCH FOR A

FOUR-LEAF

clover.

327

Treat yourself to a **TAKEAWAY COFFEE** and meet a friend in the park or next to a river; better still, stretch your legs and go for a walk. Laugh and enjoy each other's company.

328

Take a drive in a **HOVERCRAFT** for a water activity with a difference. These vehicles float on a cushion of air, so can offer a smoother ride than a traditional boat. However, be aware that they often throw up a lot of spray, so wear something waterproof and take a change of clothes.

329

Stage a NERF-GUN FIGHT at the park or in the woods. Make sure you don't accidentally involve any wildlife, and be aware of any bystanders!

330

If you're the kind of person who prefers to watch the world go by, book yourself a CARRIAGE RIDE and enjoy the scenery in a much more serene fashion.

331

Go WINDOW SHOPPING in a town or city that you haven't visited before. Choose somewhere with a lake or river running through it and you can enjoy a lunchtime picnic while you're there.

For a fitness challenge, train for and take part in
a **TRIATHLON** – a multi-discipline sport consisting
of swimming, cycling and running. The swim
element often takes place in open water like a lake.

333

To train for a triathlon, you need to be competent
in *all three disciplines* – it's wise to find a club
to train with. If your triathlon involves open
water then you'll need a wetsuit. Other essential
equipment includes a bike suitable for the terrain,
and a really good pair of running shoes.

☞→ **334** ←☜

Go for a country walk and **SAY HELLO** to everyone you
see. Being sociable may lead to a new friendship.

Breathe in

THE SALTY
SEA AIR

AND FEEL RESTORED!

☞→ **336** ←☜

If you use a computer to **WORK FROM HOME**,
set up in the garden on a pleasant day. If you don't
have outdoor space, work near a window and throw
it open to the elements – bring the outside in.

☞→ **337** ←☜

Join in with **CHILDREN'S GAMES** in the garden
or at the park. Who says we all have to
act our age 100 per cent of the time?

⇒→ 338 ←⇐

For true daredevils, how about taking a **RACING CAR** for a spin? Off-road experiences give you the chance to try out different terrains and a range of vehicles.

⇒→ 339 ←⇐

If you had a childhood dream of being a heavy machinery operator, then **DIGGER OR MONSTER-TRUCK DRIVING** is a chance to get to grips with something bigger.

340

It may sound obvious, but for either of these activities, you'll need to be able to drive a manual vehicle. As with any driving experience, always *listen carefully to the safety instructions.*

➤➤ 341 ⬲

There's no reason that board games or cards can't be played outside in the LOCAL PARK. Pack some snacks, drinks, your favourite game and a pack of cards, and head out into the sunshine.

➤➤ 342 ⬲

You don't need to have the talent of Claude Monet to produce a work of art. Buy a paint-by-numbers kit or set up an easel at the beach or on the riverside, then produce your very own MASTERPIECE.

⇒→ 343 ←⇐

A **COLOUR RUN EVENT** – where colourful powder is thrown at runners as they take part – can get quite messy, but the memories and the photos will last a lifetime.

⇒→ 344 ←⇐

Head to the beach and take a volleyball and a net with you. Find some space, mark out a court and **PRACTISE YOUR RALLIES**! Your net could also double as a badminton net, so pack your shuttlecock and rackets too.

⇒→ 345 ←⇐

ATHLETICS CLUBS are always on the lookout for keen new members. Whether you're a runner, a long jumper or skilled with a javelin, training outside on a track in the fresh air could be just the ticket for your next outdoor adventure.

ICE CLIMBING is not for the faint-hearted. However, if you're a climber looking for a real winter adventure, it could be the challenge you're seeking. Ice climbers typically scale facades of frozen waterfalls or other vertical surfaces, while roped, using ice axes and other equipment to help them up. Beginners will start with a shallow incline and build up to a steeper grade.

347

Do some research online first and *chat with other climbers*. There are quite a few online forums and Facebook groups. In terms of equipment, you'll need ice boots, axes, crampons, a helmet and gloves. These can often be rented or purchased second-hand.

348

LAND SAILING involves steering a type of wheeled yacht with a sail. The "yachts" are usually built with DIY kits, and then sailed with other like-minded enthusiasts. You should practise first in an open empty space, like a long stretch of beach.

349

When you're land sailing, *wear a helmet as well as knee and elbow pads* just in case your yacht flips. To reduce the chance of this happening, aim to keep your speed down.

350

Enjoy some aerial acrobatics at an **AIR SHOW**. Marvel at the impressive displays and skill that's involved.

– 351 –

Stage

A PLAY

IN THE FOREST.

⇒→ 352 ←⇐

If you have a work meeting on the agenda, take it outside and turn it into a **WALKING MEETING** – you'll probably find the fresh air and exercise will bring forth more ideas.

⇒→ 353 ←⇐

Conquer a fear of heights by finding a **ROPE BRIDGE** to walk across. Take someone with you for moral support if you need to!

⇒→ 354 ←⇐

When you're dining out, opt for an **OUTDOOR TABLE** at a restaurant or café and watch the world go by at your leisure.

⇛→ 355 ←⇚

If you have an interest in engineering, how about designing and building your own box car? Once you've finished building, you could enter your creation into a **SOAP BOX DERBY**. There are lots of resources online with details on how to build a box car and kits are also available. It makes a great family activity.

356

Wearing a helmet is probably the *number one rule* of box car racing. You are, essentially, speeding along in a home-made vehicle. Take it on some test runs first on a large, flat piece of ground to make sure you can safely turn, control and stop.

Wrap up warm and go along to a firework display.
Enjoy the **COLOURFUL SPECTACLE** and soak up the
atmosphere with a warm drink and some food.

358

Purchasing and setting off your own large
fireworks in the garden can be risky; it's
always best to *attend an organized firework
display* and feel safe in the hands of experts.

Build an **OUTDOOR MARBLE RUN** in your garden
from bits and pieces you have at home and the
things you find in the natural world. Sections of
wood, cardboard tubes, leaves, pebbles and egg
boxes can all be put to good use. Then have fun
sending marbles or ping-pong balls down the run.

⇒→ 360 ←⇐

You don't need a large campfire to **TOAST MARSHMALLOWS**. You can do this over a barbecue or a fire pit in your garden, on your balcony or in some parks and beaches. Take some biscuits too, and make s'mores. Enjoy them with a relaxing glass of wine, or a cup of steaming tea.

⇒→ 361 ←⇐

Whenever you're out walking a normal route, **LOOK UP** as well as ahead. Sometimes we can find beauty where we've not thought to look before.